ALSO BY DR. JAYÉ WOOD

Poetry

Platinum Love

Strength of a Woman

Fiction

Cement Rainbow

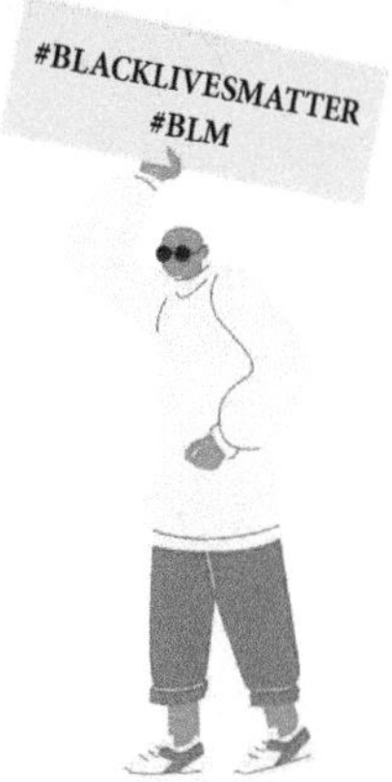

DEDICATION

To Black Lives Matter (BLM), Justice for All (JFA) and an immediate realistic, positive, non-symbolic change for all society!

CONTENTS

PART TWO: DREAMS AND RAINBOWS

PART THREE: GOD DON'T LIKE UGLY

ACKNOWLEDGMENTS

Thank you God
for your continued **grace, compassion, guidance, and love!**

Thank you: Mom
for doing the best that you could, where you were and who you were. I shall always treasure what we shared during the last decade of your life. Oh, the **beauty of true forgiveness!**

Thank you: Dad
for in spite of your challenges, you always encouraged me to achieve my dreams and rise above the status quo. Though you are no longer here, I see your smile and **feel your spirit!**

Thank you: Lisa
for designing the graphics for this book. Yes, I know you sometimes were unsure of the direction to take.
Then one day you said, **"It's already in the universe!"**

Thank you: Damita
for the editing of this book. I remain **infinitely grateful!**

Thank you: Michelle
for writing the forward to this book; your kindness is **immeasurable!**

Thank you: Matthew
for assisting me with the picture collage. I remain **appreciative!**

Thank you: Aunt Mat
for the nearly thirty years we shared together (joys, sadness, tears, challenges, and more). Equally as important: Our acquired love and respect for each other! Thus, I shall always treasure sharing your last days and moments on this earth. I can still hear you whispering in my ear as you held me tight with such calm and serenity, "I love you, take care of … for me!" **Your request has been honored.**

Thank you: In memory of

Shangé Dee Poo (Manchester Terrier Mixed, 12 years) who often laid on my lap or bed as I wrote! What comfort, smiles, and joy you always gave to me and others to include children! Then came **Lady Coco** and **Sir Prince**, (Chow Chow's, 16 years) both given to me as gifts. Told nobody wanted them. Well, my royal babies, you not only served as a companion to me but also as therapy dogs for nursing homes. In addition, you received many certificates and awards for your services. **My heart still warms** each time I think of you all! Surely, you are my **Just in Time Smiles** and I shall forever love you!

Thank you: **Yesterday's Peaceful Warriors of Equality**
upon your shoulders I stand and hope within my writings:
I inspire others to model the grace, dignity, peace,
and kindness **you so eloquently typified.**

Thank you: Readers
for taking this **poetic journey!**

FOREWORD

The powerfully written words of Dr. Jayé Wood in *He Is My High* speaks boldly to the human state of mind, the plight of mankind. Cleverly worded, each poem offers gold nuggets and glimpses into life's journey, the paths through which we all must travel. The emotions that loom in our consciousness including health, wealth, love, acceptance, joy, and pain are all well-captured here. The author so eloquently disseminates some antidotal advice for life's pitfalls. It is indeed a guiding light of hope during today's time of chaos, deaths, violence, protest, and riots in response to the continuum of societal injustices regarding race, justice, and equality for all. The author offers cheers and kudos to those of us who are experiencing the ever-fleeting, much sought-after emotion of the mountain top high.

Dr. Wood's book profoundly makes known that regardless of our differences, we all have the desire to feel love and inclusion. Yes, the author is spot on! This yearning is woven throughout our DNA. It is the strongest force on earth. We enter this world demanding love, approval, and affirmations from those around us. Yet, as permeated throughout this magnificent collection of poems, in its attempt to perfect us, life quickly begins to serve us a series of customized highs and lows.

Dr. Wood unquestionably has a very moving and captivating poetic voice of substance, character, realism, compassion, and strength. The author's poetry spans decades, reminding us that true transformation is not only a process but must also first start within! The author's words capture the essence of the human mental transactions. This book is intrinsically spiritual, emotional, compelling, and offers something for everyone to embrace during these most challenging times. The author of poetry undoubtedly echoes: HE is Love regardless of our diversities, and we are all equally entitled to His High.

Michelle Reese-Wiseman
Owner/Principal Mortician
Wiseman Funeral Home & Chapel, Clinton, MD

PART ONE

POWERFUL

HOW SEXY!

I

love the person that

I continue to become—unlike some that

say they dislike getting older—this hang, this

sag, this thinner, this spread, etc. etc. etc. just not the

Same

and yet, sometimes if one would honestly reflect

their younger years—they may discover not only immaturity

naivetés, self-loathing, low self-esteem, and even a false sense of

Self

oh, but the joy of maturation with

confidence, style, and elegance—how sexy indeed, so free

to be and do you—with such purpose, understanding and

Reassurance

that you not

only made it, but

for His grace, continue—to

Be…

BE THE POWER

When

you feed into negativity

you merely fuel its

Energy

why not be the

power using your given

keys

to start and stop

your engine—forcing negativity

To

back up—make a

U turn and stay

In

their lane—how sweet

God's gift of self-

Control

when one understands

the ultimate switch is

He…

RUBBER BAND

(Dedicated to Dr. Savage)

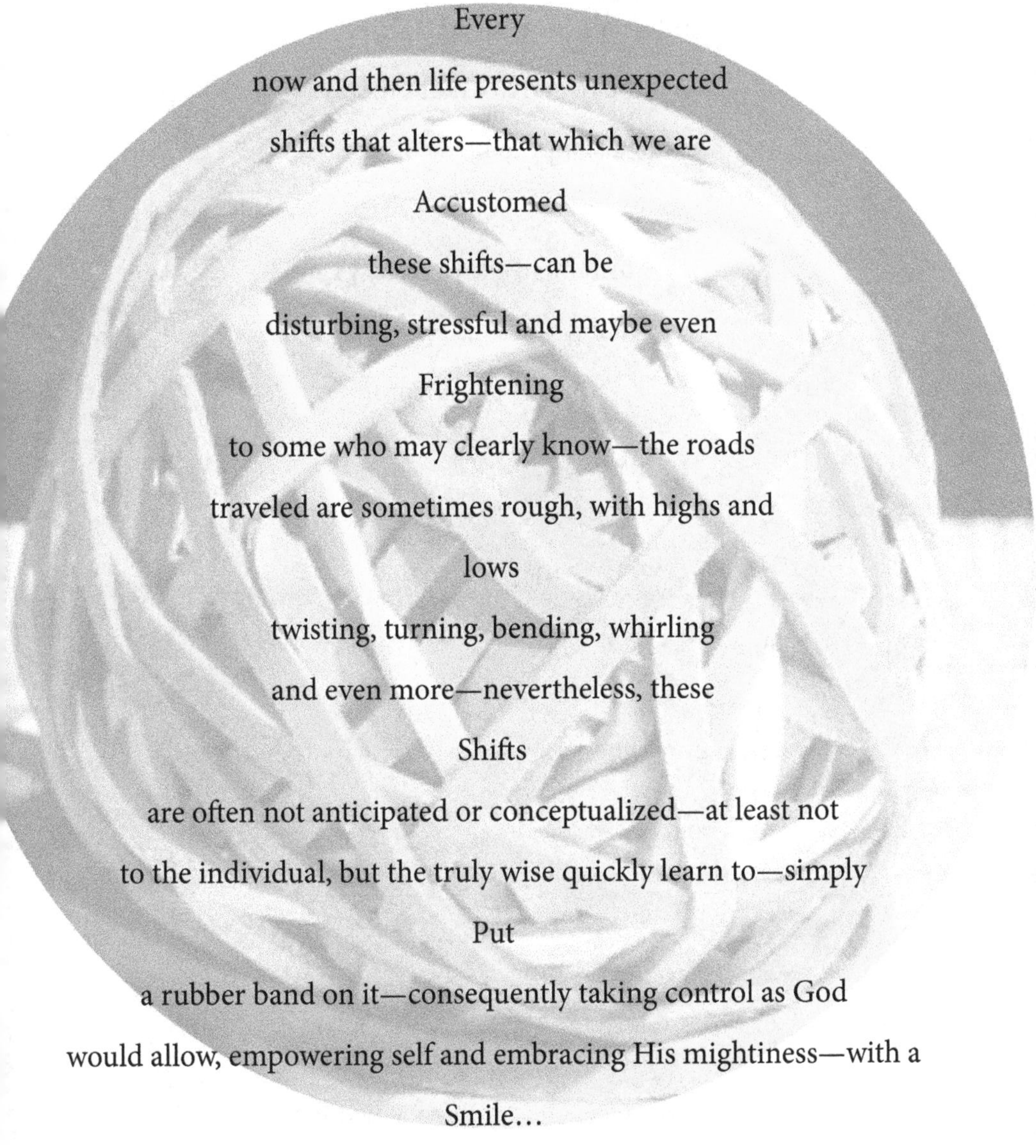

Every

now and then life presents unexpected

shifts that alters—that which we are

Accustomed

these shifts—can be

disturbing, stressful and maybe even

Frightening

to some who may clearly know—the roads

traveled are sometimes rough, with highs and

lows

twisting, turning, bending, whirling

and even more—nevertheless, these

Shifts

are often not anticipated or conceptualized—at least not

to the individual, but the truly wise quickly learn to—simply

Put

a rubber band on it—consequently taking control as God

would allow, empowering self and embracing His mightiness—with a

Smile…

SPIRITUALIZE

Don't

internalize—instead, spiritualize

the negativity that others

attempt to place upon

You

use the negative energy

of naysayers as stepping

stones—a gift from

God

when people are against

you they resent that

you have arrived beyond

Yesterday

thus, even when people dislike each other and

have thrown stones at one another—they will come

together when their collective intimidation towards you is

High

oh but, when God

empowers us with strength—He

also protects and guides accordingly...

NATURALLY

When

someone enters your

space and or

you theirs—it

should happen

Naturally

because you want

to be—instead of

feeling obligated

to fulfill the

Expectations

of other people in

shadows—unlike God

when needed He simply shows up

with an illumination of—His true

love…

POWERFUL

When

you love God you can forgive

another who has caused—much

Pain

when you love God—you can

seek His guidance and welcome His

Lead

when you love God—your heart must demonstrate the

ability to forgive even the most challenging and atrocious

Behaviors

surely, the capacity to forgive without any malice and or

hidden agenda is one of the most powerful expressions of —God's

Love

and each time you forgive, it brings you closer

to becoming the total person God created you—to

Be

remember forgiving does not necessarily mean forgetting

instead, it reveals one's character, ability, and faith—to

Grow…

HEAVY LOAD

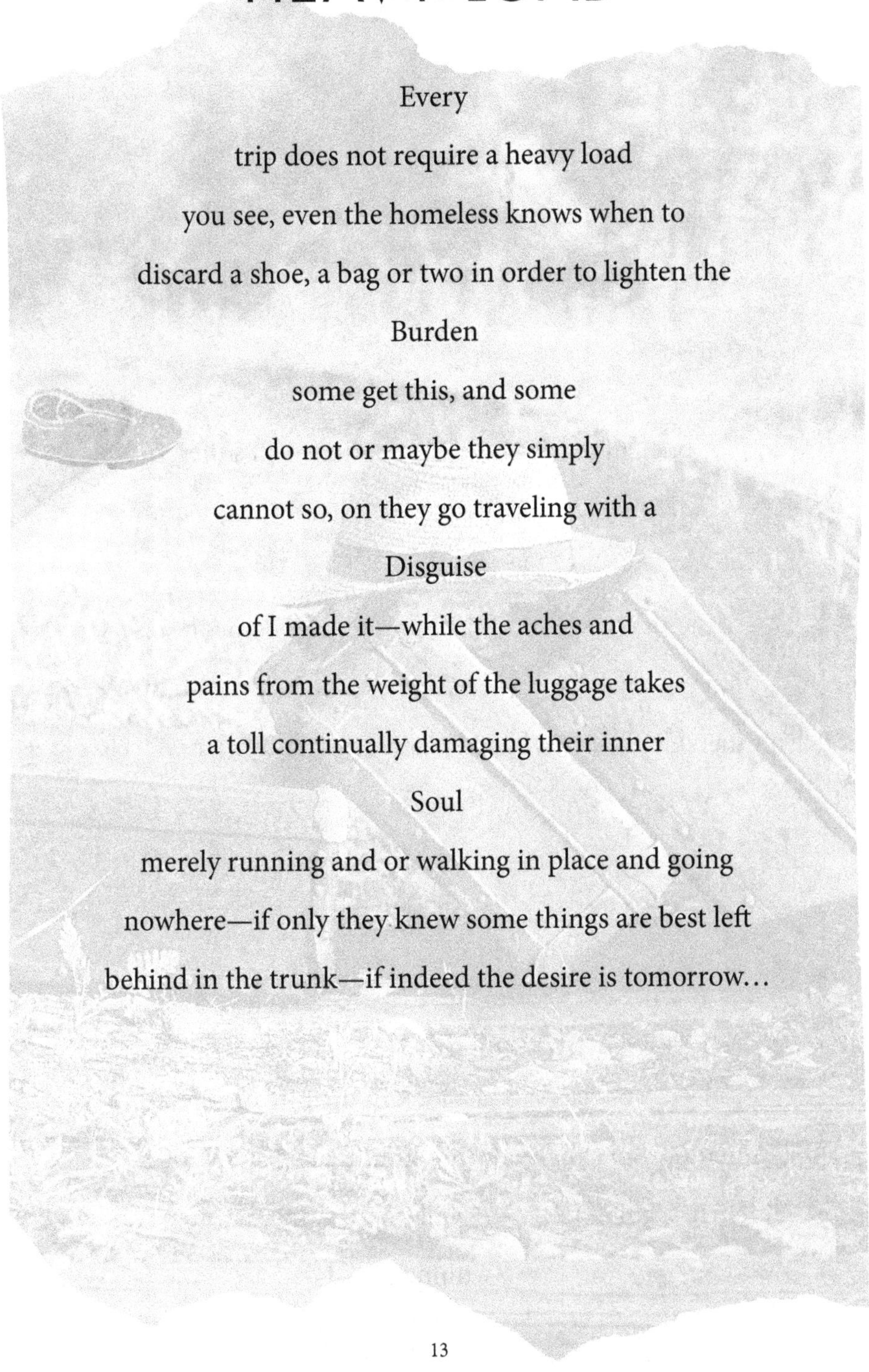

Every
trip does not require a heavy load
you see, even the homeless knows when to
discard a shoe, a bag or two in order to lighten the
Burden
some get this, and some
do not or maybe they simply
cannot so, on they go traveling with a
Disguise
of I made it—while the aches and
pains from the weight of the luggage takes
a toll continually damaging their inner
Soul
merely running and or walking in place and going
nowhere—if only they knew some things are best left
behind in the trunk—if indeed the desire is tomorrow…

SELF

Healthy

relationships begin with

self and when nurtured, protected, and fed the

right nourishment it enhances its sustainability and

Beauty

on the other hand, when

one fails to do this their relations will suffer

sometimes leaving them empty, lonely, angry and

Broken

so, the next time you think, and or hear someone else

utter or even shout—I have no relationship with my

mother, father, sister, brother, and other family etc. etc. etc.

Because

they did, they said

see you don't know

but they, and on—and on

If

indeed, one dares to just look in the mirror—gently

inhaling and exhaling while simultaneously asking for

His sincere guidance—they will find the answer often reside

within…

HE IS MY HIGH

Whether

I am on God's

mountaintop or in

the low depths of His

valley—He is my

High

oh, but indeed the mountain tops

are magnificent and unmatched

flaunting its gloriousness, extravagances

and illustrious illuminating silky velvet carpet

Welcome

is its doormat—nonetheless: Be

advised there are no lotteries or free tickets

to the mountain top instead, one must embrace the

valley's challenges which often include hard work and

Perseverance

this is the healthiest high

no bad ingredients, illness or any other

toxins—just His love, guidance, grace, blessings

and a guaranteed addiction that you will Grow…

FORGIVENESS

When

people say I already asked

God's forgiveness—I do not owe

anyone else anything—yes, I have

Demonized

wrongly criticized and

just outright lied to get what

I needed, shucks—even the

People

who joined me—knew it

was a lie, nevertheless, they

now felt falsely empowered to

Destroy

someone we all quietly

envied and secretly—wished

to be, what was—I supposed to do

Well

my response is simply

do you believe in—God

and prayer—if so, to receive

Forgiveness

you must do more than pray—and

wait for the chicken to show up at your

door cleaned, fully cooked, and ready to eat

You

must take responsibility, be accountable

and your acts must include giving from

your heart—it is only then God will return these

Blessings

to

your

heart…

GIVE IT UP

When

you are angry

you're stuck—full of hatred

Intoxicated

suffocating, evaporating

slowly and then increasingly

Overwhelming

are the gasses—of your

negative energy—caught in a

Trap

sometimes for years you may wonder not

sure, not caring just living your life in a

Hurricane

a self—imposed prison that

only you can free—your

Soul

so, let go—give it up and waste

no more —sit up, stand up and reach

Upward

determined to connect with His gracious love and

claim the freshness of a new emergence—of you…

GRATEFUL!

I

am grateful for so many things

where do I begin, how do I count—the

Stars

I suppose, first merely for

being yes, that I am—and that I

Exist

oh, to be—to be

in His infinite love and

Grace

which makes possible for all the wisdom—I have

acquired—that is clearly reflected in my continued

Growth

which echoes the uni-sonic walk my soul and spirit

embraces at each awakening and to Thee—I give all the

Glory

and—I say

Thank You!

THE DAWNING

(Dedicated to Mom, Ms. Irene, and the Barnes Family)

When
God sends for
an angel—He
does not ask
He
simply chooses
without consultation
the best to join His
Premier
team—sometimes
He might send
notification to the
Chosen
unfortunately, some do not
receive this well and thus, may
go into denial, panic and even ask:

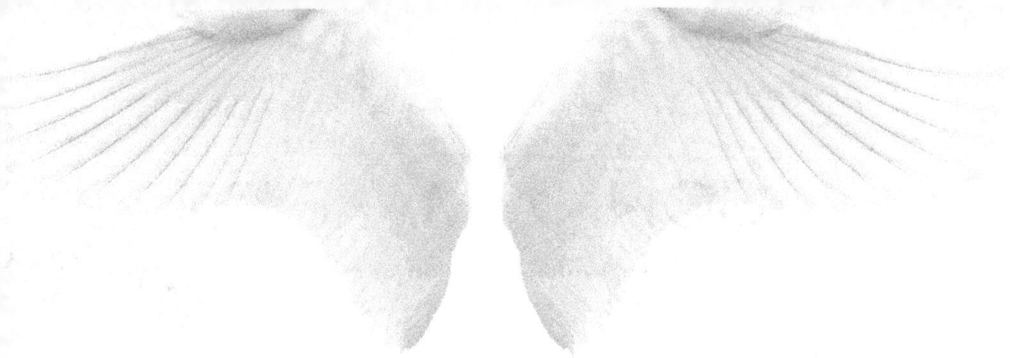

Why

me, her, him etc. and or more time—oh

but, for those who know and love Him clearly

understand that the reality of His selection—is not the

Extinguishing

of the light, but

the dawning of a new

Amen! Amen! Amen!

GONNA MAKE IT!

(Dedicated to a younger self)

Been jumping
been bumping, been walking
been talking, been screaming, been
dreaming, gotta make it—gonna make it
Somebody help
just a weep or peep, just
a sip or tip, just a slice or
crust, gotta make it—gonna make it
Somebody must
I've begged, not even an egg, I've
prayed, only turns gray, I've cried—until
I am tired, gotta make it—gonna make it
Somebody please
I tried, now I
must hide my
pride, gotta make it
Gonna make
it—somebody
hear me, somebody
somebody—somebody!

SERENITY

I
sit alone in Her embrace
comforted by its—holy
Face
Her—voice I
speak and inhale thou
Breath
I love Her serenity
and—adore its
Beauty
like a dear friend we
have become and our time, I
Treasure
and kiss the heart of Her soul
each time we meet causing my
Spirit
to evolve as does
the night—uninterrupted
Into
day—good morning
my almighty, my savior, my
Grace...

ACE

When

one has a desired

destination to pursue—it

must be consistent with what they

Believe

thus, it is essential

that one not only visualize

but have sustainability for its ultimate

Embrace

therefore, even when faces

are smiling it is imperative

at all times—to be steadfast

Vigilant

indeed, the devil's mask

includes a many—envy, hatred

etc. etc.—all aimed at shutting you

Down

nonetheless, you not only

hold the power, but His—trump card

which is permanently marked He—is the highest

Advantage

of any and all who dares to

interrupt His will so, remember to keep Him close and

play it not like bingo—no lucky number to cover instead, let

God

be

your

ace—in the hole...

BOUNDLESS BEAUTY

My
daily sunrises are
awesome—each
greeted with a kiss of
kindness, encouragement and
Guidance
I need not ask—He
simply knows my mind
spirit and soul, gentle is
His Lead—and yet, very
Profound
to know this kind of
love, I have not always known
oh, but to withhold the boundless
beauty of His flowers today—is priceless and
Immeasurable
even as I retire to rest
from a sometimes—weary day
my sunsets are breathless—as
I lay within the warmth of His
Embrace...

PART TWO

DREAMS AND RAINBOWS

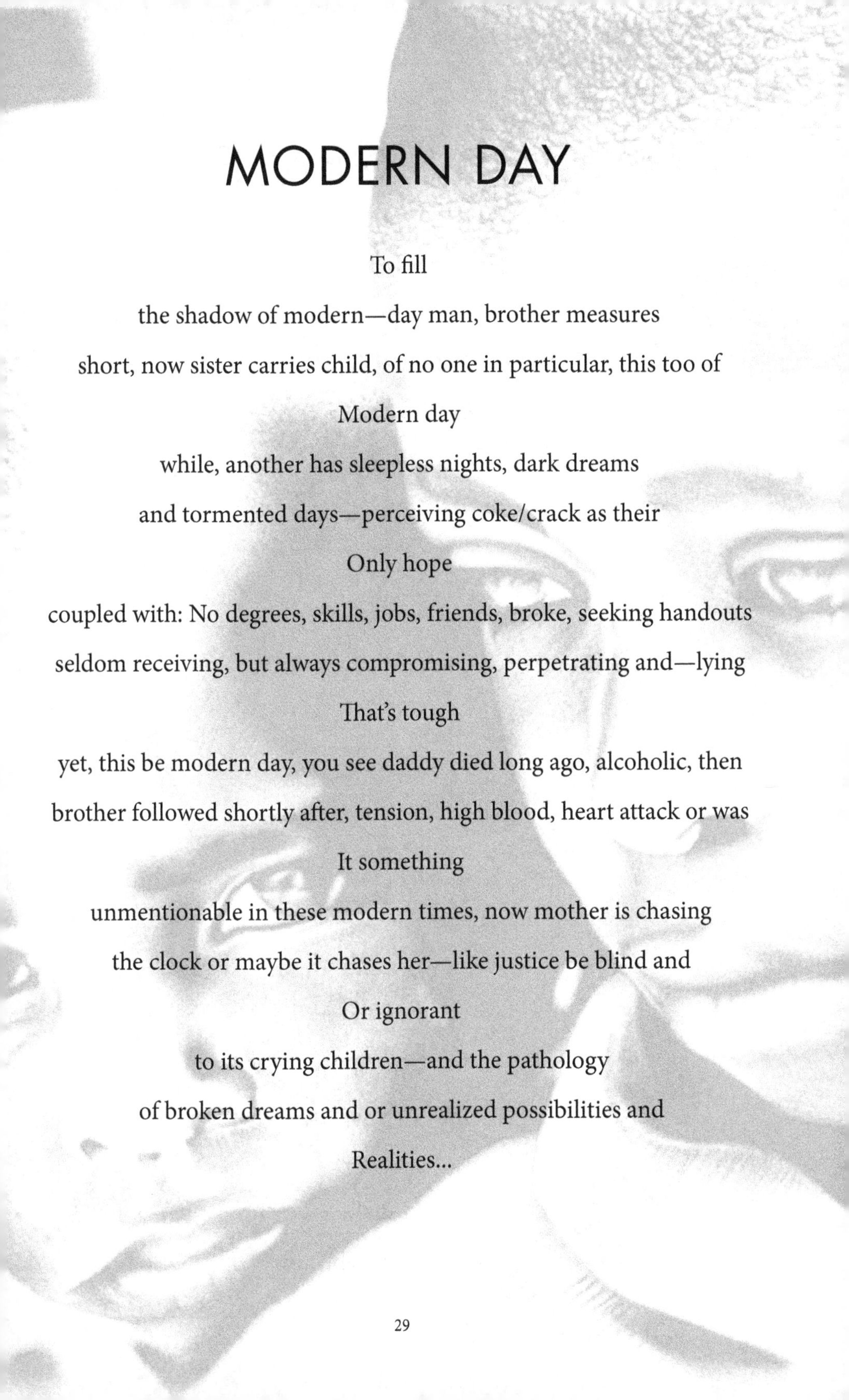

MODERN DAY

To fill
the shadow of modern—day man, brother measures
short, now sister carries child, of no one in particular, this too of
Modern day
while, another has sleepless nights, dark dreams
and tormented days—perceiving coke/crack as their
Only hope
coupled with: No degrees, skills, jobs, friends, broke, seeking handouts
seldom receiving, but always compromising, perpetrating and—lying
That's tough
yet, this be modern day, you see daddy died long ago, alcoholic, then
brother followed shortly after, tension, high blood, heart attack or was
It something
unmentionable in these modern times, now mother is chasing
the clock or maybe it chases her—like justice be blind and
Or ignorant
to its crying children—and the pathology
of broken dreams and or unrealized possibilities and
Realities...

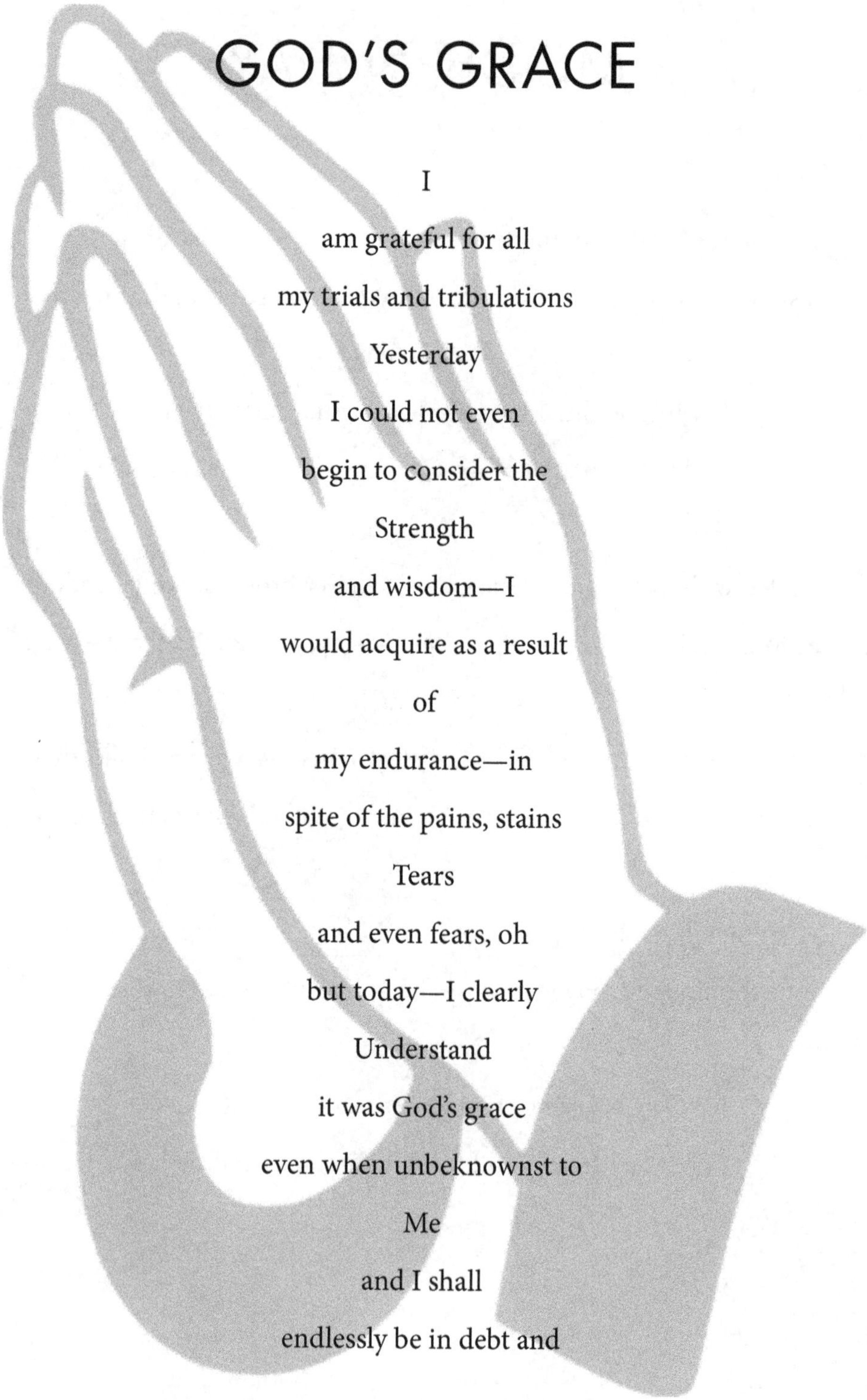

GOD'S GRACE

I

am grateful for all

my trials and tribulations

Yesterday

I could not even

begin to consider the

Strength

and wisdom—I

would acquire as a result

of

my endurance—in

spite of the pains, stains

Tears

and even fears, oh

but today—I clearly

Understand

it was God's grace

even when unbeknownst to

Me

and I shall

endlessly be in debt and

Grateful

for His presence, persistence

unconditional love, and compassion

Forever...

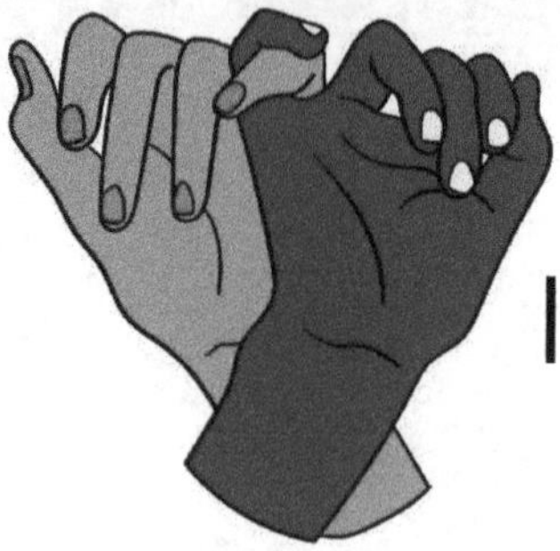

IMAGINE THAT

(Dedicated to Sister Linda)

When there
is true sisterhood—there is friendship and the
spirit of its beauty shines in the presence of others
No matter
what the challenge when there is a mutual desire, plan and
a "we can do it" attitude all imagined dreams—are realized
This coupled
with a deep respect, trust, and understanding for each
other—fosters a profound kinship that is unbreakable
Surely, this
is a gift from God—that must be nurtured, treasured and shared
to hopefully, allow the universe to embrace its sweetness, kindness and
Glorious garden
of diversity and to be able to not only—imagine this, but
know that its magnificence—is the result of love, compassion
and Him...

FREE

Ego
can be a good thing when it propels us to succeed
on the other hand, it can be a bad thing—when it causes us not to
accept our bad behaviors and own up to our true feelings behind them
Unfortunately
when this occurs, our bad ego persists causing a
disintegration of self which leaves us—imprisoned within
our created trap of bitterness, anger and a disguise of blame
Regrettably
if we do not stand up today with a sense of
importance and urgency for our wrongs—imploring damage
control later may be impossible therefore, asking for sincere
Forgiveness
without any hidden agenda and or some great
embrace from those we have harmed—will set our spirits
free and allow us to breathe and be the freshness of a new day...

A SMILE

The

house is quiet and

so, too is the remembrance of

their pain, I know mine will also

soon fade, but today—it still hurts

Solidarity

all alone it seemed

when a memory invaded

my space and within the

rapture—of its embrace I

Smiled

while simultaneously giving

thanks to God and letting go, clearing

my mind, no longer feeling left behind

funny how something as simple—as a smile, can

Help

one—shine

just

in

time...

A MIGHTY VOICE

(Dedicated to a young Sugar Baby)

Unprepared
underdeveloped and uninformed—even as a
teen, just a kid nonetheless, the mother to be no longer
A mother
today, I am—what to do
maybe PA (Public Assistance) at least just for now
The father
some said, gone to join the military—while
others chuckled saying—yeah, singing in jail
Oh, well
Mom's in and out, daddy's drunk, siblings are divided and the
pathology is high yet, nowhere to go, so here I'll have to stay—my child
And I
nevertheless, I'll go back to school, get some training, earn
a degree, find a good job, a decent place to live and she'll
Grow up
to be a happy child—just maybe
with some luck—I thought and then
I heard
a mighty voice say: Know thy God, let Him be your guide, believe, take
responsibility, be accountable and your dreams shall exceed, because He Is and
He Can...

DREAMS AND RAINBOWS

Dreams
must be awakened
in order—to be
Realized
far too often, people
do what they do and
Consequently
end up where they are
wondering what happened and or
Why
I suppose for some the answer is
simple—in other words, to know the
Beauty
of His Rainbow—is not enough
instead, one must understand its
Evolution
thus, dare to not only dream—of
a rainbow, but embrace its fruition as well...

CELEBRATION

Birthdays and
holidays come once
a year but, finding
a—true love may only
happen once in a lifetime
And so,
I celebrate each day by
thanking God for our love
compassion, friendship and the wisdom to
know this—gracious blessing is to be shared
Thus, as
we gather this year with family, friends and
even a few strangers in celebration of His birth
we must pray not only for that we can touch, feel
and see, instead—for the hope of eternal love for
All people
not just in our devotions on the
calendar Christmas, instead engraving the
love, we have for Him in our hearts, souls
and spirits—as an everyday celebration stamped
lifetime...

WHO AM I

Throughout this very
diverse universe thousands of young
people have probably asked themselves these
questions before: Who Am I, What Am I—and
How can I
particularly for those who grew up in settings where the norm was crimes
jump out boys (police), drugs (addicts/dealers), prostitution, back alley
abortions, number backing, baby mama drama, daddy gone etc., could
Be very challenging
and so, within the echoes of one's mind as they continue to mature
even more questions, and conversation—with self, may include: Is it
true, before every success there's a failure if so, I have had my failures
Where is my success
is it true: You must start
from the bottom, before you can
reach the top—if so, will I ever
Reach the top
is it true: You should be a good
sport even when you lose if so, I have
been a—damn good sport, will I ever

Be a winner
is it true: It is better to
give than to receive if so, I
am tired of giving—when will
I start receiving
is it true: If you reach out and take
a hand, you can make a friend, if so, I
have reached so many times, but—where
Are my friends
is it true: The Lord
works in mysterious ways if
so, when will—He do something
Mysterious for me
and then, by the grace of God as one continues to
grow along the way—and is receptive to change, they will
learn trust, respect, belief in Him and how to dream beyond
Dreams, stand taller
than their stature, work harder and reach past the clouds
for His awaiting hands: Who Am I, I made it—I did it, and
I now reach for you, God's beautiful child—yes, you can too...

ONE STEP

When

sickness, broken

hearts and or other

tragedies occur one's

Response

to how are you

doing—is likely to be

I am taking it one day at a

Time

surely, this can sometimes be too

much so, why not take it—one step at

a time—with God's grace and guidance

Consequently

better ensuring that

your bounce back will indeed

be stronger than your —setback...

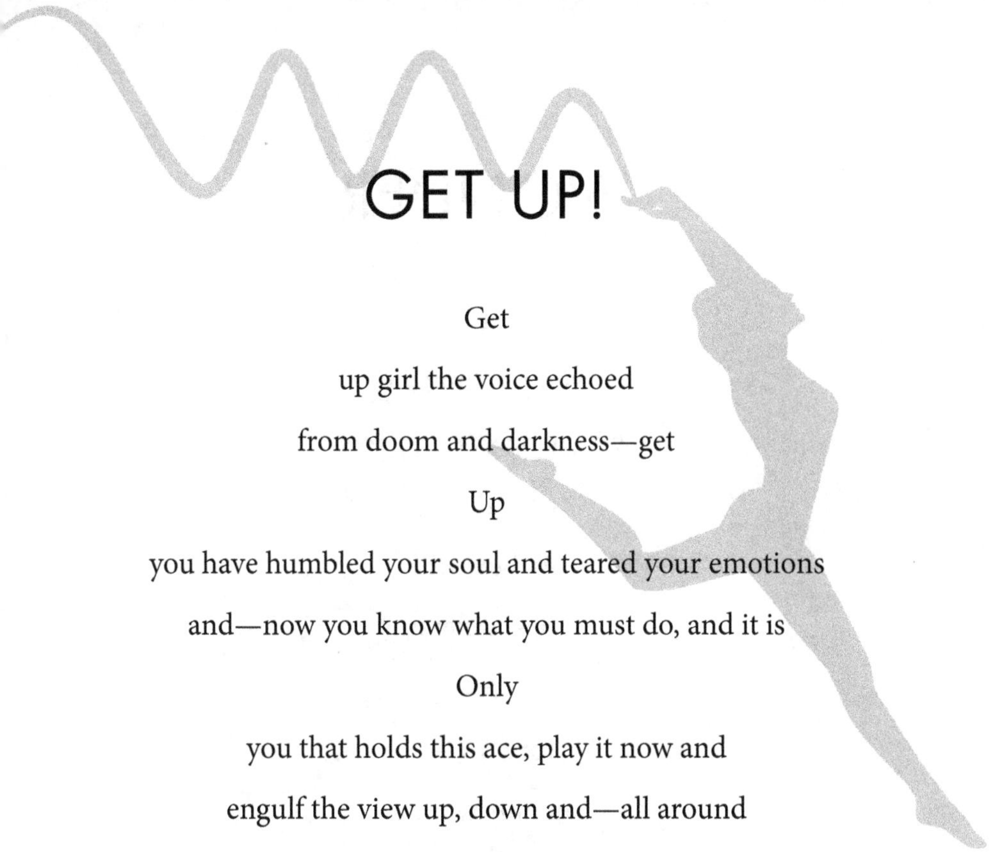

GET UP!

Get

up girl the voice echoed

from doom and darkness—get

Up

you have humbled your soul and teared your emotions

and—now you know what you must do, and it is

Only

you that holds this ace, play it now and

engulf the view up, down and—all around

And

so, together lifted by Him with the spirit

of His mighty love, my heart and soul were

Strengthened

with such profoundness

consequently, today—I rise again...

WONDER

I

wonder if my life

will change—tomorrow

If

so, how will

it be—different

Yes

for now—I

can only wonder

Who

what, where

I—will be

How

will I—face the challenges

and will I rise above—today's

Injustices...

NOTHING

(Dedicated to BLM and JFA)

I

saw a man running

I heard a man scream

I said nothing

I saw a man get shot

I saw a man die

I said nothing

I saw the murderer

I watched him run away

I said nothing

I heard a policeman ask for evidence

I saw the policeman look for clues

I said nothing

I watched the wife cry over her husband's dead body

I saw two children clinging close to the woman's dress tail in tears

I said nothing

I who have been taught: See and don't see

I who have been taught: Hear and don't hear

Who am I

I saw nothing

I heard nothing: I said nothing...

FOREVER

Wanting

to pinch the moment—forever

visibly displayed upon my cognitive wide

screen permanently set on long term and yet

It

was not the first

time that I saw you, instead

it was the final time that I

Loved

you—your presence, your essence

and your mere being—yes, it was at this

moment that I knew this was a reflection of

God's

love which is a constant validation that every day He presents

a gift if only a moment to treasure, appreciate—and when we do

even many years later a—forever moment can remain as vibrant as its

Beginning...

BE WONDERFUL

I

do not want to one day

be gathered amongst the

yesterdays—and wondering

about my life's should haves

would haves, could haves or if's

Instead

I want my life's

performance to be awed

upon for its character

integrity, compassion, kindness and

love of Him—consequently, influencing

Others

to be wonderful

and understand

this is the only way

one's—true purpose in

life can be validated...

CHANGE

Today
I was given the gift of life
and I receive it with joy, love and
Hope
in spite of the ongoing systemic racism and
injustices that continue to be the norm—we must
Change
yes, this disease of hatred with its
very deep roots must be eradicated
Immediately
while, at the same time honoring and
respecting the many who fought for justice and
Equality
oh, indeed, this can be and will be a mighty challenge especially
when there has been so much pain, stains and tears, but in—this
Moment
if true change is to happen it must happen now—no more
rationalizations, demoralizing, minimalizing or mere symbolism

Together

we can, yes, we must stand united towards our

common goals—this is the only way we can bring an

End

to the status quo, so

I challenge any and all—who dare to

lead

the charge—with dignity, pride, grace and compassion

to bring about a very much, long overdue, much needed

Transformation...

BITTER SWEET

Some-days

life is vulnerable

you can feel everything

Some-days

you feel nothing

simply numb

Some-days

life seems fair and then another

time you draw the short straw, oh well

Some-days

there are things you

want to know—and then

Some-days

those same things you wish you did not

know—secrets and lies indeed, bitter sweet

Some-days

feeling safe to share ones hopes, prayers, dreams, pains and fears

seem nonexistent mainly between people who profess to love each other

Some-days

yes, this can be lonely oh but, when you know that

you can call God's 911 everyday, all day—you got a friend...

PART THREE

GOD DON'T LIKE UGLY

STOP THE HATE!

(Dedicated to BLM and JFA)

Some are
asking—how do we stop this epidemic
of progressive hate—that knows no single prejudice and
has become more the norm then the unexpected rarity and, so
A few
are saying, it is simply the sign of the times
and it is what is—thus, do the best you can to be
safe and protect your loved ones and that's about all you can do
Oh, but
more and more are saying—we must teach and practice compassion
not conspiracy, giving not taking, embracing differences not belittling
or attacking and complimenting achievements of others, not sabotaging
Consequently, there
will be an increase in accepting
knowing, loving and being oneself—which
appears to be a void—amongst the violence
Indeed, change
is a process, nonetheless, if we dare to start this transformation
today—what a blessed rainbow to behold with Him centered amongst
its diversity of colors, electrifying, captivating and simply saying—I
Am pleased...

Injustice

is

not

just—a

Black

issue, instead

inequalities

impacts—all

People

yellow, brown, green, blue

purple, white, trans, gay, disabled, old

young and the like—thus, whether one

Silently

sits, stands—watches

walks or runs in place

in its presence—this kind of

Complicity

merely co-signs

validates and permits the

continuance of hatred, bigotry and

Condemnation

towards God's very diverse

rainbows: Yes, until true respect can

be given in totality to all its colors—He

Frowns

and as is His

will—God will

hold thee—Accountable...

GOD CRIES

When

a child is used

as a pawn—it is abuse

and God cries because this

Child

is His gift—not

only to parents, but the

grandparents and others in their

Village

to nurture, cherish and

share without malice or revenge

thus, when a child is used as a

Pawn

for control—the one holding

the child believes foolishly and or

through ignorance that they have all the

Power

and the favored one in—the child's

eyes and maybe for now, while—deceitful they are

nevertheless, when a child is used as a pawn behind anger, this

Disguise
quickly becomes very transparent
it simply never works, because one day the
child grows up and then realizes that they have been
lied
to and deprived of relationships with others who love
them now consequently, resenting the exact one who thought
they had all the power unfortunately, they did not—and do not
Know
God's mighty
supremacy and so, as
always, in His—time
He
will prevail
with a simple
I—got this...

DEATH MONEY

When

someone thinks of you

in such a blessed way, while

preparing their journey home, you feel

gratitude, especially when what you gave them

came sincerely from your heart and soul with no

Expectations

nevertheless, sometimes

this same someone may

decide not to include and or gift

another as they did you—oh, hell

indeed has no fiery to match death

Money

particularly when one

feels entitlement just, because

not only are they angry, but

shouts loudly to any and all—that

they perceive are listening and or can be

Influenced

endlessly, ranting and raving

I am birth, well they are too, but they do

not know them like me, as a matter of fact—they

do not love them like me, and I know that they did

not like them that way etc. etc. etc. Maybe I should

Contest

what, I don't know, just because—I feel hurt

and my heart aches well, I know—I should have

been there, should have called, but they should have

called me, told me—shucks, I thought they would get

better nonetheless, I think, and it ought to be me after all—I

Am...

UNFREEZE

When

somewhere else happens

at your front door—in

your house, the pain can be

devastating—with a forever

Stain

leaving you wishing

upon each sunrise—for a fast

sunset, then He gracefully steps in to

simply remind you to—breathe and

Unfreeze

your heart—suddenly, the

possibilities and realizations of

fresh air, budding flowers and

butterflies are everywhere and you can

Now

open

the

front—door...

CONSUMED

Your
time is spent day after day, weeks on end months
and now years refusing to hear His voice—you are so
Consumed
with self, so angry, so mean, and so hateful that there is
no way for you to ever have a real relationship, while your
Initial
presentation may sometimes exude charm, interest and caring
the real you—quickly surfaces when you feel as though you are
Losing
control, someone dares to have an opposing thought and or is bold
enough to tell you—you are wrong, without taking a breath like a
Bat
out of hell raging, spurring vulgarities with antagonistic insults
you become exhausted and twice as mad, because your audience
Tires
of your unchanged rhetoric and simply says enough, nothing or just
walks away, your pain—you cannot hide, it is very visible, and it
Stains
us all—maybe the truth
lies within—your shadow...

THROWING STONES

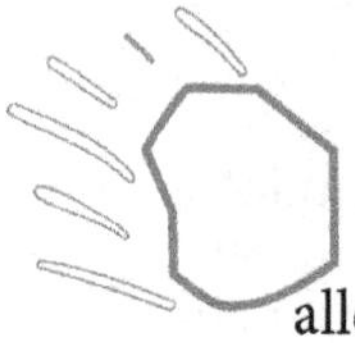

When the

messenger refers to the persons

allegedly viciously attacking you, your

character, integrity etc. as they—and then when

you ask: Who are they and the response is something like

I am just saying, I was there, but I—did not say anything

Be aware

disengagement at this point may be

necessary unfortunately, the nameless they

at this point is questionable and possibly simply

does not exist, in other words, often the messenger in this

case is undeniably the one—throwing stones and hiding

their hands

remember: God is

not anonymous—when

He

exists

within...

TOXICITY

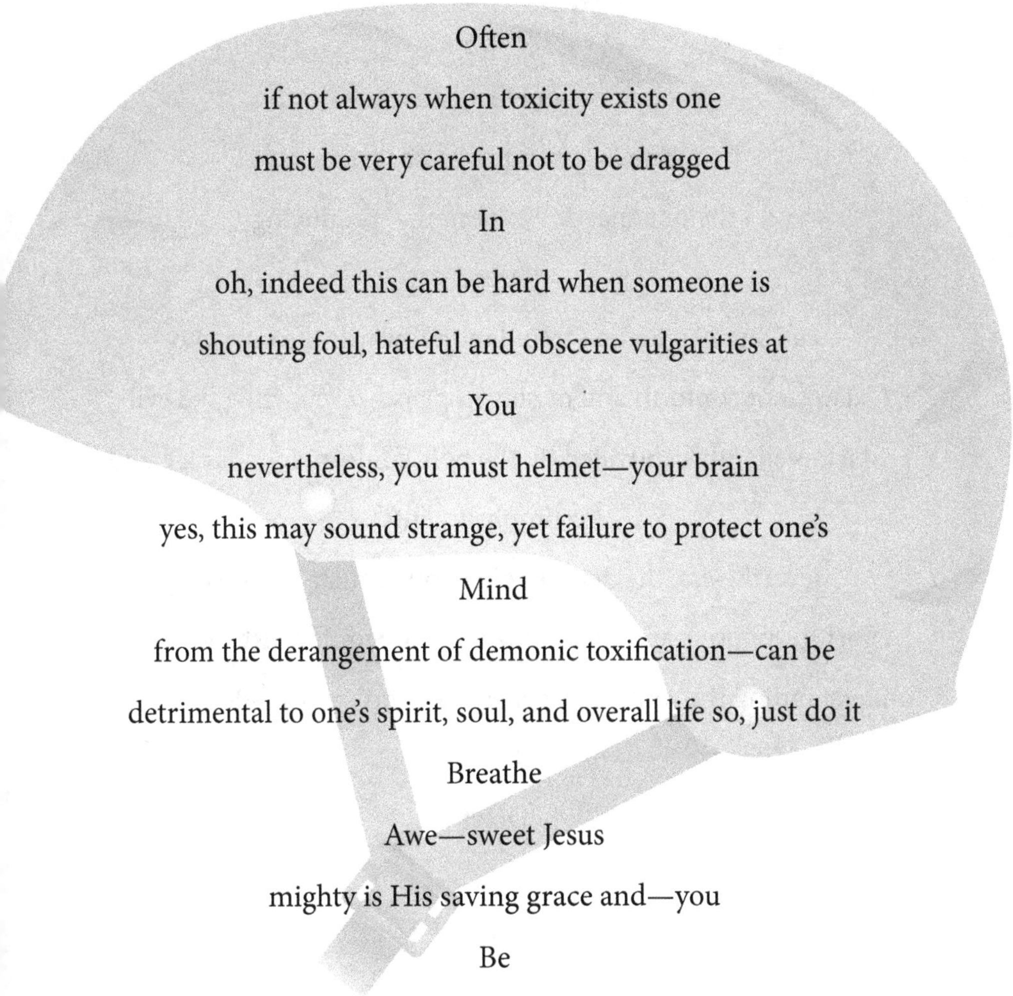

Often

if not always when toxicity exists one

must be very careful not to be dragged

In

oh, indeed this can be hard when someone is

shouting foul, hateful and obscene vulgarities at

You

nevertheless, you must helmet—your brain

yes, this may sound strange, yet failure to protect one's

Mind

from the derangement of demonic toxification—can be

detrimental to one's spirit, soul, and overall life so, just do it

Breathe

Awe—sweet Jesus

mighty is His saving grace and—you

Be

The

Taller...

GOD DON'T LIKE UGLY

Envy

fascination and fear cause the devil

in some to attempt to rise up against

the one that does not fit in—producing

Dread

causing heightened trepidation towards the one who

dares not conform and or stay in place—even while the evil

spirit is silently captivated by the non-conformer's courage and

Accomplishments

nevertheless, the demon will continuously make every

effort to suppress and demoralize the nonconformist, clearly not

understanding the route of the blessings and or just—do not believe

God

Don't

Like

Ugly

Consequently

as wise spirits know—what goes around

comes around, sometimes immediately and sometimes much

later, but always: You see, it is already stamped—guaranteed to

Expire...

DRUNK IN EMOTIONS

Some people
are drunk within their emotions subsequently, they
become addicted to irrationalities which —impacts
Decision-making
consequently, blaming others while simultaneously
disregarding the warning signs, even when—boldly shouting
Danger ahead
instead, propelled by their intoxication and an
obvious need to destroy—by any means necessary, on and on
They go
swirling from lane to lane with a false sense of control, jumping in
the face of anyone who dares to talk above them and or has the nerve
To interfere
some may say: They are simply a maniac
crazy, delusional and or high—on something, when
In reality
if one travels without—God
collisions, wrecks and even fatalities
Are destined
thus, maybe the warning signs
should read: Be Aware — God Ahead...

IGNORANCE

Impulsivity
appears to be related to
immaturity and thus, reveals
Ignorance
which can go—unnoticed
at least until you see it in
Action
yes, ignorance may be
safe if she or he does not
Speak
oh, but if they do, undoubtedly it will disclose
a lack of validity in their information, and or a
Failure
to explore positivity
related to learning new things
Consequently
it is very hard if not—difficult to reason
with ignorance particularly when coupled with
Stupidity
and yet, some appear surprised when ignorance is in charge—saying
often whispering to others, things like: I cannot believe they made that

Decision

how did they get to be in charge, who put them there, oh well, change

will not occur by tossing pennies in a wishing well, blaming, instead

Prayer

with belief, sincerity, acknowledgement and

accountability to—move forward is now needed, then

He

will provide guidance—allowing others to use the wisdom

of their experience as the foundation—to make better and or

Great...

DECEIT!

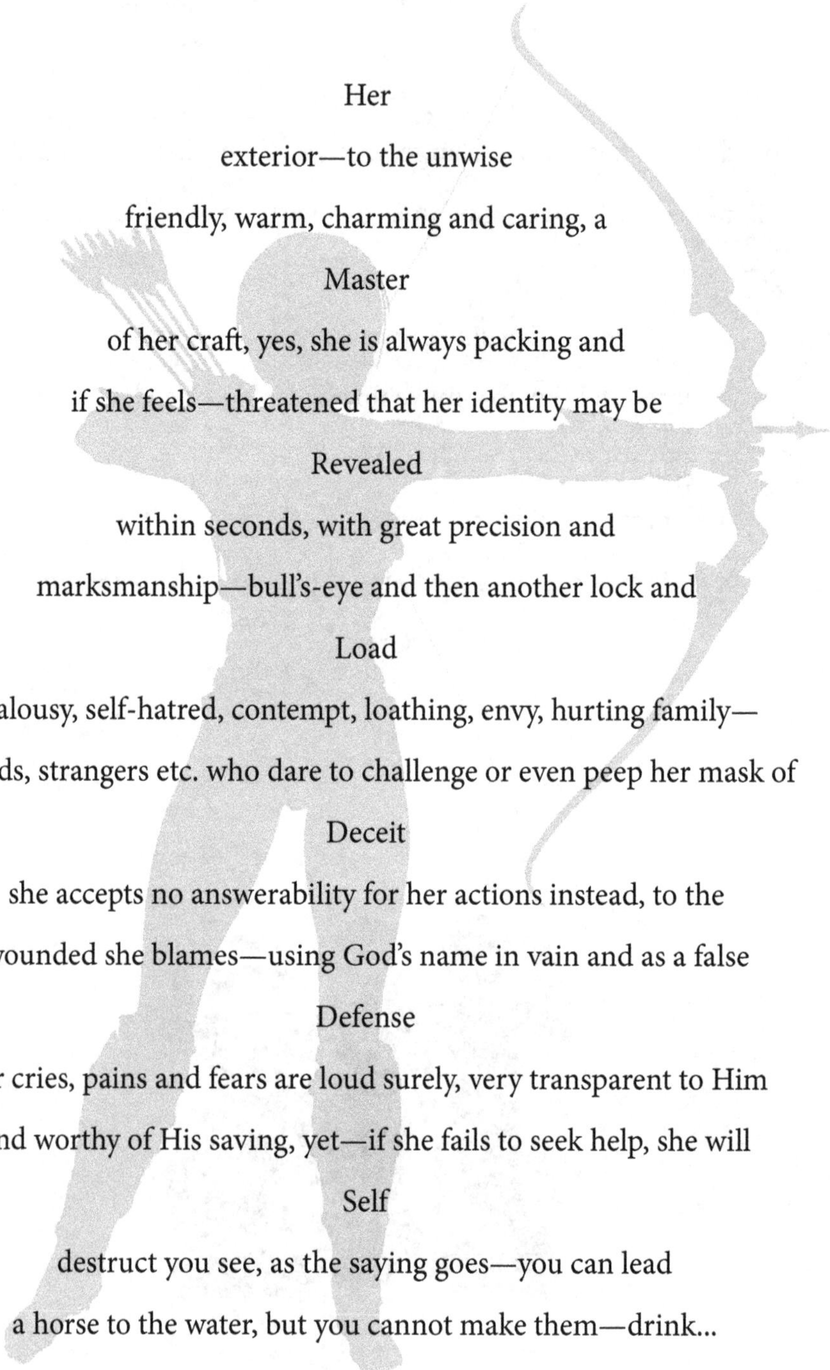

Her

exterior—to the unwise

friendly, warm, charming and caring, a

Master

of her craft, yes, she is always packing and

if she feels—threatened that her identity may be

Revealed

within seconds, with great precision and

marksmanship—bull's-eye and then another lock and

Load

jealousy, self-hatred, contempt, loathing, envy, hurting family—

friends, strangers etc. who dare to challenge or even peep her mask of

Deceit

she accepts no answerability for her actions instead, to the

wounded she blames—using God's name in vain and as a false

Defense

her cries, pains and fears are loud surely, very transparent to Him

and worthy of His saving, yet—if she fails to seek help, she will

Self

destruct you see, as the saying goes—you can lead

a horse to the water, but you cannot make them—drink...

DARK LOYALTY

When

people are scared they go

to what they believe to be their

safe place, oh, but when it is not

Unbeknownst

to them it will

surely, slowly—if not

quickly become their worst

Nightmare

while falsely giving

them their—moments

desire and at the same time

Tarnishing

every relationship

they have, had and

hoped to have—equally as

Devastating

who they are, might have become, dream to be, all

shattered and yet, their dark loyalty prevents them from

knowing or even reaching for—His always present royal guidance...

BURNING

Holding
on to the past
making assumptions—just
burning up, not wanting to ease the
Pain
and or extinguish its very
destructive flames—now wildly
running out of control as one continues to
Harbor
some memories of many
a yesterday's—yes, they have told the
story for so long, that even when given accurate
Facts
that their recollection
of an event—past life
happenings are indeed
Flawed
they may choose to continue to be angry, because if
not, to face evidence, realities—that will reveal their recall never
happened that way, would erase—the justification for their burning
Fiery...

UNWELCOMED

Sometimes
the hurt and pain never really goes away
even when you think you have left it—in the
Past
when in reality—it comfortably
resides just below the surface of your being
Unwelcomed
yes, this tenant pays no rent and yet, there is no
expiration—thus, will boldly show up at any time
Unannounced
and very vividly displayed upon its face, are the ugly
tattoos of a past devastation, with its many trials and
Tribulations
of—a
very challenging
Journey
you traveled, while, sometimes feeling so alone, because you
stood up to—the status quo, the devil and his wrongdoing, you said
Something
you did something—and with
God's magnificence, you made—a difference...

CHARADE

Some
people spend their entire life blaming
others for their failures, mishaps and other
predicaments—due to their bad life choices
and yet, these pointing the blame fingers may
even appear strong and confident on the surface
Nonetheless
far too often, lurking below the surface of
their being is a lot of hurt, pain and continued
self-hatred and so, in an attempt to hide and or not
accept their weaknesses they practice transference—by
accusing others of lying, not being trustworthy, caring or loving
Unfortunately
they become skilled at this craft and lure others in with
fake emotions, friendship, trust and continued lies, their behavior
is Academy Award worthy, best actress/actor: And so, today they get the
trophy but, tomorrow its shine and glimmer will surely fade and they
must now work twice as hard to keep up—their charade, you see the

True

honor of love is

earned, treasured and it takes

quite a man or woman to self-reflect

and know when to seek help, then and

only then will they know—God's grace and

Mercy...

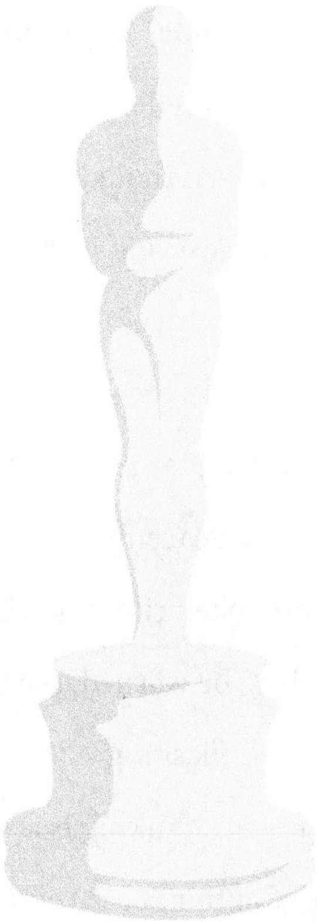

FALSE EXPLOSION

During

this present climate of pandemic

some have said—it is a false sense of

Revelation

while others have expressed we have

been here before—and once again, our voices

Conversations

are loud, public, visual

and—echoes across all

Media

yes, even though we

are up close and in their

Face

some folks are saying it

does not matter if protest are

Peaceful

or provoked riots and the

like thus, be warned, see the

Flashing

light ahead—its blinking is a warning

sign saying: Caution, be careful of a false

Explosion

of opportunities/reform for those viewed as underprivileged

wrong complexion, gender, geographic, nationality etc. etc. etc.

Indeed

this may be so, and yet, I

believe—and so too must you

God

did not bring us

this far, for us—to turn back

Now

so, as a people, as a society, as in unity, we must

not merely stand together, but collectively, we must

Vote

in order to ensure

the American Dream of

Justice

for—all

is—a reality!

AFTERWORD

Over the past decades, God presented many trials and tribulations in my life. Some were life- threatening; others included the loss of lives and more. Yet, I never stopped writing. As a matter of fact, these challenges made me stronger, and just when I began to breathe—to write this book, there was the no knock killing of Breonna Taylor, the pandemic (COVID-19), death of George Floyd, Black Lives Matter (BLM), murder of Rayshard Brooks, etc., etc., etc. And then, there were the deaths of two mighty trailblazers, Congressman John Lewis (Good Trouble) and Justice Ruth Bader Ginsburg (Notorious RBG).

Quickly, upon my mental wide screen, my mind reflected on so many other pioneers who not only sacrificed their lives but demonstrated with grace, peace, compassion, and integrity their true commitment for equality and justice for all of society. Yes, I was a young teen, young adult growing up in Washington DC during these historical times—that we now reflect on today.

And so, I knew I must not just continue my writing but move now to publish this book. The inspiration for the poems compiled in this book are ones I wrote a many of yesterdays as well as today. Some have expressed to me that all of the poems in this book are very applicable to current times as if I had written them today. Then others have asked. "How do you do this?" Well, the answer is really simple—you see,

He

Is

My

High

"Always a Poet!"

Dr. Jayé Wood

HERE'S WHAT FOLKS ARE SAYING

Dr. Jayé, your poems are inspiring and uplifting. They give a voice to many of the struggles and challenges we face today, reminding us that there is a higher power that we can turn to for hope and relief! I so needed to read your work! My life has been **ENRICHED** by your poetry! A call for love and unity pervades throughout your poetry. I will buy/gift this book to others! **Thank You**!

—Joyce, Washington, DC

This book is encouraging, uplifting, thought-provoking, and very much needed for such a time as this. I enjoyed all the poems: Touched on the human emotion, regrets, complexities, realities, resilience, and most of all the Hope, Grace, Mercy, and Love. A few of my favorites are "God's Grace, Spiritualize and Heavy load." I enjoyed this poetic journey immensely and will be buying this book for family and friends. Dr. Jayé, your poetry is authentic, transparent, a blessing, and you are **a GIFT to society!** God bless you!

—Yvonne, Clinton, MD

The poems featured in *He is My High* are so relevant to today's times. It is hard to imagine that some of these poems were written very early in the author's life. While I love and felt a connection to all the poems, there were a few that touch me deeply, based on my own experiences and personality such as "Powerful." I personally sometimes have a hard time forgiving in its entirety, but after reading this poem, I will do better! Two others were "Nothing" and "Change." Not only does the author's poetry exemplified all the racism and violence going on in the black communities and overall society, it **speaks loudly to hope, strength, unity, and change**! Dr. Jayé, your poems are **AWESOME**!

—Joleen, Suitland, MD

I am an Eritrean-American who had the pleasured and honor to participate in a curbside read of this book. Immediately, upon opening the book, my fellow doctor and I could not stop reading these **electrifying** poems. The author's ability to touch humanity and keep it alive through her poetry is **AMAZING!** A generous gift to people of all different levels of society. The author's poetry is not only very relevant but also so vibrant, colorful, edifying, insightful, thought- provoking, well-written, and easy to read. I love them all! Just to mention a few: Imagine That, God Don't Like Ugly and Stop the Hate! I am gifting this book to my team. For inspiration during these trying times, each day before the doors open, we will recite a poem from *He Is My High*! Clearly, the author demonstrates through her poetry a **heart touching** of all stages of society, as well as nature that is really needed and in great demand in our communities. Dr. Jayé, **A Blessing** you are! **Much applause!**

—Dr. Debretsion, Fairfax, VA (licensed veterinarian)

I really enjoyed reading this book: I relate to these poems and like that they speak to what's going on in the world today with the current civil unrest. One of my favorites, "The Dawning," gives me a smile when I think of my deceased grandfather. "Nothing" makes me know the importance: See something (injustice), Say something and **I will**! **GREAT** book to read anytime/anywhere!

—Jade (16 years old), Upper Marlboro, MD

I love these poems so much! While reading I often shouted **Hallelujah** and **Amen!** The author's poetry is such a source of **strength, inspiration, and wisdom**! If one's heart ever needs uplifting, these will be the poetic words of life to you. God gave this author a mighty platform to teach, guide, and inspire others through her poetry. Dr. Jayé you are a **Great Woman of God! Thank you** for this **spiritual journey!**

—Pastor Steele, Clinton, MD

This book has a **MAGICAL** effect on me. "How Sexy," I felt this one! It's so me. I enjoy the aging process: Know who you are, what you like and don't like. "A Smile" (a simple smile can make someone's day), "Nothing" and "Powerful!" A book to **read again and again!**

—Linda, Largo, MD

He Is My High is a moving collection of poetic stories that has warm, funny, passion-filled, current events and nostalgic moments that moved my soul. The poem "Powerful" resonates with me deeply, as it is my present, past, and continual journey so much so that I have AGAPE tattooed in the body of my butterfly. "Heavy Load"—just **WOW!** Read it three times! "The Dawning" is my favorite. August 18, 2007 marks the day that I lost my first love, the best dad my children could have ever been blessed with. He was 31, on his way back to us when he was struck and killed by a drunk driver just two blocks from the house. This poem let me know that even in the darkest of moments, be steadfast in knowing that God will sustain you in the deep, cold, windy darkness of the valley. Just as He will guide your steps on the daunting yet beautiful journey to the mountaintop. **Thank you**, Dr. Jayé, **May God Bless and keep you on your journey!**

—Cookie, Clinton, MD

My husband and I had the pleasure and honor to attend a book reading: *He Is My High*, Dr. Jayé **gloriously MAGNIFICENT.** Awe-inspiring and relevant to today's human experience. The poetic voice of the author as she read the poems and narrations conjured up feelings of joy, hopefulness, and tears: A **Brilliant** work which speaks to the depths of humanity. It **inspires** us to nourish our spirits and provides a blueprint for developing the self-assurance to endure hardships, overcome adversities, and resist the noise of negative temptations. It also reminds us to be grateful, never to lose sight of the God-given light within us, grounds us, and validates who we really are, "God's precious children." This book is a **MUST READ! Thank you for sharing your talents and loving spirit!**

—Dennis and Pat Millsboro, Sussex County, DE

MORE PRAISE FOR THE AUTHOR

Dr. Jayé Wood has been and is an inspiration to many. Today's books call for new ways of thinking, providing support for those that are going through a struggle or just providing insights on things to come. *He Is My High* does that and more; this collection of poems is perfect for the current times we are experiencing with the many social injustices that are occurring. This book is **AMAZING!** A definite **must-read** for all, and I am sure you will find a poem that fits any situation you may be experiencing and or have experienced. **Thank you,** Dr. Wood for always being willing to share what God has placed on your heart to continue **encouraging** others.

—Dr. Damita Goods, Vice Provost, Williamsburg, VA

As Salaam Alaikum (Peace Be Unto You).Dr. Jayé Wood's book of poems and reflections is powerful, humble, and engaging. A thought-provoking and heartfelt message to the mind, body, and soul. This book is a call to the **Remembrance of Divine**. While reading, it is as if I made a connection to a kindred spirit. The author's sincere reflective writings are a gift of insight for the individual, the collective human soul, a oneness that God intended. A daily read and time for sober reflection. It pulsates with God's given energy, love, and devotion. **I SALUTE** the author for sharing her **poetic genius** that seeks to unite a society versus separate! **Thank You!** Dr. Jayé. **BIG PEACE!**

—Albert Sabir, Executive Director, Non-Profit Human Development, Washington, DC

Dr. Jayé Wood, renowned cultural leader, life coach, and social influencer is a **lyrical beacon of light** who employs her poetry to cast rays of wisdom and life lessons to all. This book is **awesome . . . CONGRATULATIONS!** As I retreated into this great compilation of poetic artistry, *He Is My High*, I visualized myself as a character in many of the narratives! I loved the emotional expedition, in reading all the poems to include "Rubber Band" and

"Spiritualized." In this simplistic presentation, I encountered **extraordinary** revelations about the uniqueness of life and the power of the human experience. I most certainly enjoyed reading this **wonderful** book and believe you will too! **Thank you**, Dr. Jayé, for summarizing your collective soul experiences into a tangible, creative, **transcending** message for such time as this: Equality and Justice for all!

—Latarsha Jones-Dixon, Doctor of Law, Baltimore MD

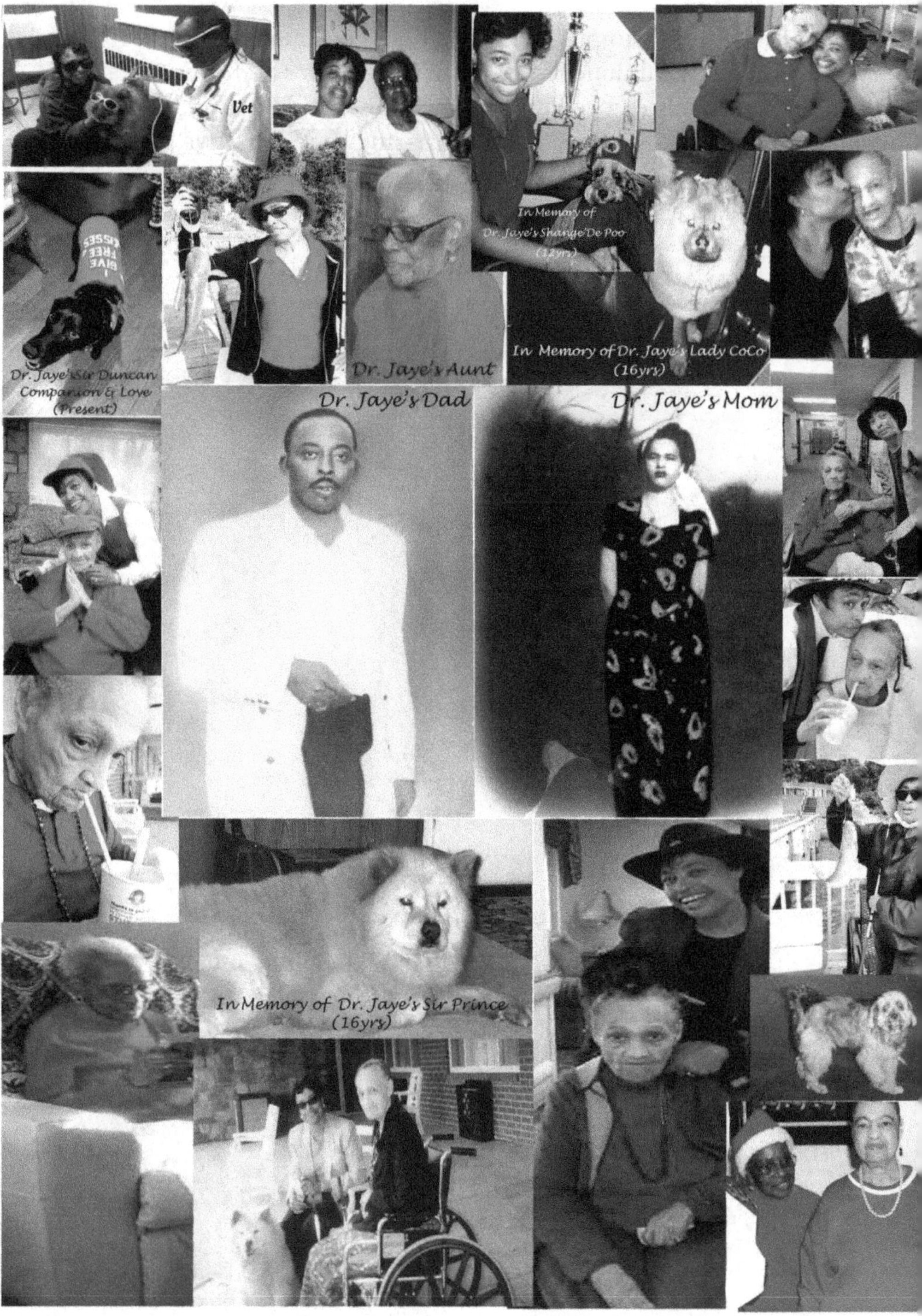
Vet
Dr. Jaye's Sir Duncan
Companion & Love
(Present)
Dr. Jaye's Aunt
In Memory of
Dr. Jaye's Shange'De Poo
(12yrs)
In Memory of Dr. Jaye's Lady CoCo
(16yrs)
Dr. Jaye's Dad
Dr. Jaye's Mom
In Memory of Dr. Jaye's Sir Prince
(16yrs)

ABOUT THE AUTHOR

Dr. Jayé Wood is indeed a very fascinating individual: strong, compassionate, and kind. Her mere presence personifies elegance, dignity, and confidence! After publishing her previous books just as she was finishing another, her mother was diagnosed with dementia and her aunt, who she had been assisting over the years, had failing health as well. At this time, Dr. Wood was not only working as a full-time professor, but also on earning her Doctor of Education in Organizational Leadership. Nevertheless, she decided to give priority to her mom and aunt. Though not publishing, she never stopped writing!

Dr. Wood soon developed a very close relationship with nursing homes, being there not only for her mom and aunt, but for other residents, staff, management, and visitors. She became a legend with the nursing home after the passing of her mom and aunt. Yes, she still supports the nursing home via visits (when safe), making donations to residents, and gifting staff for the work they do, particularly during these challenging times. Her kindness reaches out to funeral homes, persons with disabilities, and so many others!

Dr. Wood has worked in higher education as a dean and professor (organizational leadership, psychology, and criminal justice). She served as a liaison for the superior court, federal bureau of prisons, corporation counsel and attorneys. She has served as an administrator for halfway houses (correctional community facilities); a deputy warden for a very large correctional organization; a correctional training director, developing and implementing the first electronic monitoring program for ex-offenders in a very large metropolitan city; an acting general assistant to a mayor; a program analyst for persons with disabilities; a lead trainer after September 11, 2001, for Homeland Security/TSA, traveling around the country and training airport screeners; a founder and CEO of her own training company; a motivational speaker; and a presenter. She is the recipient of numerous other degrees and certifications, including counseling, pyrotherapy, and municipal management.

Dr. Wood remains compassionate about education and believes that equal education for all is essential to the overall societal success. Thus, she continues inspiring and encouraging others to reach beyond their dreams, to escape pathologies, and to not waste time and energy blaming and being stuck in the past.

Dr. Wood is undeniably a highly energetic, educated, motivated and positive person who has made and continues to make a difference in the lives of all who have had the privilege to be in her presence! As a person of color growing up in the ghetto (hood), with no mentors or resources, her achievements not only continue to astound many, but leave them in awe, as she defied the odds of being a person labeled as underprivileged, with little chance of becoming, doing, or being anything else! To the contrary, she has risen above all the stigma and continues to inspire others to be their own advocate—and then reach for someone else!

Dr. Wood is an advocate for homeless and rescue animals, particularly dogs. Most of her dogs are obedience trained and have served as therapy dogs for nursing homes. In addition, she loves walking, reading, nature, and fishing, and is quite a fisherwoman! She gives away and or donates all fish caught to others, including families, friends, nursing homes, essential workers, churches, funeral homes, and strangers. She believes her kindness reflects His strength and grace.

I LOVE HEARING FROM YOU!

Over the years, I have received many positive responses to my poetry from readers. I am always pleased that my poetry serves as inspiration, healing, affirmation, and relaxation for so many. And I welcome your positive comments. Comments may be used for publication; therefore, please indicate at the end of your comments, "You may use for publication."

Please send comments to:

Dr. Jayé Wood, Always A Poet,

9134 Piscataway Road P.O. Box 2069

Clinton, MD 20735

email: alwaysapoet0920@gmail.com

website: alwaysapoet.com

CPSIA information can be obtained
at www.ICGtesting.com
Printed in the USA
BVHW090045270621
610166BV00001B/1

9 781644 843673